Welcome to the Autistic Community

Autistic Self Advocacy Network

The Autistic Press
WASHINGTON, D.C.

Cover illustration: Lar Berry

First Printing, 2020
ISBN-13: 978-1-938800-08-5
Library of Congress Control Number: 2020904974
The Autistic Press
Washington, DC

Contents

CHAPTER ONE

To Start

Autistic people are different from non-autistic people in a lot of ways, and that is a good thing!

This book will help you understand autism. Reading this book will help you learn what being autistic means, and it might help answer some questions you have about autism. It can show you how to make life better for autistic people.

The first chapter of this book says how the book works. This chapter talks about:

- What the book is

- Who the book is for

- How the book talks about autism

- How to read the book

- What is in each chapter

You can find more resources related to this book at **autismacceptance.com.**

Who Is This Book For?

Anyone can read this book, but this book is mostly for autistic people. This means *all* autistic people.

Some of us have an autism **diagnosis**, which is when a doctor says you are autistic. Some of us have a **self-diagnosis**, which is when you figure out that you are autistic. Some of us aren't sure if we are autistic, and that's okay. Lots of autistic people aren't sure at first, and this book can help you figure it out.

People who aren't autistic should also read this book, since this book can help people become better **allies.** Allies are non-autistic people who want to help autistic people.

All sorts of people can be allies, like friends, family members, and people who work with autistic people. Anyone who wants to help autistic people can be an ally.

Most of this book will be good for allies to read, and there is one chapter of the book just for allies. It talks about how allies can help autistic people. Even if you aren't autistic, you can learn a lot from this book.

Lots of people don't know they are autistic. Some allies might actually be autistic, and you might be one of those people. This book can help you learn about yourself.

How to talk about autistic people

This book uses certain words to talk about autistic people, and we use these words for good reasons. We use words that respect autistic people, and words that autistic people chose to talk about ourselves. Some people use words that make autism seem like a bad thing, so we use words that show what autism really is.

"Person-first" language and "identity first" language

There are 2 ways that people talk about disability: person-first language and identity-first language.

Identity-first language means that you say the disability first, then you say the word "person."

"Autistic people" is an example of identity-first language. We say "autistic" first, and then we say "person." "Disabled people" and "Deaf people" are other examples of identity-first language.

Person-first language means that you say the word "person" first, then you say the disability.

"People with autism" is an example of person-first language. "People with disabilities" and "people with intellectual disabilities" are other examples of person-first language.

People can choose the words they like to be called. Many people with intellectual disabilities like using person-first language, and they've used person-first language for a long time. They want others to know that they are a person, and that their disability is only one part of them.

A lot of Deaf people and autistic people like identity-first language. They feel like their disabilities are a big part of who they are, and want others to know that their disability is important to them.

This book uses identity-first language to talk about autism. This book calls autistic people "autistic people", and not "people with autism".

The words we use might not seem important, but they are very important. The words we use change how we think. Person-first language gets used to hurt autistic people. It says that autism is only a small part of us, and doesn't make us who we are. But autism is a big part of our lives, and is an important part of who we are!

Not every autistic person uses identity-first language, but a lot of us do. Different people use different words for different reasons. You can use whatever words you want to talk about your disability!

Functioning labels and support needs

This book doesn't use "**functioning labels**". Functioning labels are words that try and show different "types" of autism, such as:

- "High functioning"
- "Low functioning"
- "Mild autism"
- "Moderate autism"
- "Severe autism"
- "Classic Autism"
- "Asperger's Syndrome"

Functioning labels don't help autistic people get what we need, because they don't show how autistic people need help with different things. Functioning labels hurt us. Someone might say we shouldn't get help if we are "low-functioning", or that we don't need help if we are "high-functioning".

This book uses the words "**support needs**" instead. Support needs are things autistic people need help with. Different autistic people need help with different things. Some people need more support, and some people need less support. Some people might have more support needs sometimes, and less support needs other times. The words "support needs" mean we need help, and don't judge us for needing help.

This book does talk about groups of autistic people, like non-speaking autistic people and autistic people with intellectual disabilities. These words make more sense than functioning labels, and are also more respectful.

How To Read This Book

Here are some tips for reading this book:

Chapter names are big and bolded, and start with the number of the chapter.

For example, the first chapter is called "Chapter One: To Start".

Chapters are split into sections to make them easier to read.

For example, right now you are in the section called "How To Read This Book"! The topic of each section is split up with big bold text.

There is a list of other things to read at the end of each chapter.

These extra things can help you learn more about what we talked about in the chapter.

Keep track of Words to Know.

This book will have a lot of words that you might not have heard before. Words that you should know will be written in **bold**, and we will say what the word means the first time we say the word. There is also a "Words to Know" section of the book, so if you forget what a word means, you can look at this section for help.

About The Chapters

Chapter One: To Start

This is where you are right now! Chapter One is about the book and who it is for, and talks about how to use the book.

Chapter Two: All About Autism

Chapter Two tells you more about what autism means. It talks about things autistic people experience and what autistic people need.

Chapter Three: Who Can be Autistic?

Chapter Three talks about who can be autistic. Autistic people can have other disabilities besides autism, and this chapter also talks about those disabilities.

Chapter Four: Autism Facts

Chapter Four answers some questions about autism. It tells you the facts about autism, along with some wrong ideas people have about autism.

Chapter Five: Autism and Disability

Chapter Five talks about what disability and neurodiversity mean. It shows why disability and neurodiversity are important.

Chapter Six: Self-Advocacy and the Self-Advocacy Movement

Chapter Six talks about self-advocacy. It says what self-advocacy means, and tells you who can be a self-advocate. It also talks about the self-advocacy movement, and gives you tips about how to be a self-advocate.

Chapter Seven: Know Your Rights

Chapter Seven talks about disability rights in the United States. It shows the rights of autistic and disabled people.

Chapter Eight: Finding And Making Autistic Community

Chapter Eight talks about the autistic community. It says what autistic community is, and tells you where you might find autistic community. It also talks about who is left out from autistic community, and gives tips about how we can make sure nobody is left out.

Chapter Nine: Being An Ally

Chapter Nine is all about allies. It gives some advice about how to help autistic people. Even autistic people might find this chapter helpful, since it can be useful to help other autistic people!

Chapter One Resources

You can find the links to these resources at **autismacceptance.com/book/chapter-1-resources**

- Person First Language and Ableism - by Amy Sequenzia
- The Problem with Functioning Labels- by Finn Gardiner

All About Autism

This chapter will talk more about what autism means. How you feel about autism is up to you, but we hope this book helps you feel good about autism.

Here are some important things to know about autism. We will talk more about these things later in the chapter.

What is autism?

Autism is a developmental disability that changes a lot of parts of our lives. It changes how we think, understand the world, move, communicate, and socialize. Autism makes us different from non-autistic people, and that's ok! Autism is a normal part of life, and makes us who we are.

What's a developmental disability? Am I okay?

Autism is a **developmental disability.** A developmental disability is a type of disability that starts when someone is very young. Down Syndrome and cerebral palsy are other examples of developmental disabilities.

Most developmental disabilities are there when someone is born. Autistic people are born autistic, and we will be autistic for our entire lives. An autistic person never stops being autistic.

It can be hard to tell if people are autistic when they are very young, since most babies look and act the same. Autistic babies may not seem like they are autistic, but that doesn't mean they aren't autistic. You just can't tell yet!

Most of what we know about autism was learned by studying kids. Autistic adults don't look or act the same as autistic kids. We might learn how to look "less autistic", or hide parts of ourselves. We learn to act like the non-autistic people around us. This confuses people, so they might think autism can "go away" when an autistic kid gets older. But we are autistic our whole lives.

Developmental disabilities are normal, and they are an important part of the world. Autism is a normal part of life, not a sickness or a disease. There's nothing wrong with being autistic. It is just one way to be a person!

Autism changes how we live our lives. Sometimes, autism might make things harder, but there are also lots of good things about being autistic. We wouldn't be the same people if we weren't autistic. We can be proud of who we are.

How Autism Works

You might hear people call autism a "spectrum". That means that every autistic person is different. We all like and dislike different things, and we all need help with different things.

Some autistic people may need a lot of help with one thing, while other autistic people may not need help with the same thing. One person may look "less autistic" than another person, but there is no such thing as being "more" or "less" autistic. We are all just autistic.

For example:

> Renee is autistic. She is non-speaking, and uses her iPad to communicate. Renee lives alone. She can cook and clean her house by herself, but she needs some help going out to get groceries.
>
> Percy is autistic, and can talk. Percy lives with a support person. He can't cook or clean his house by himself, but Percy can go out to get groceries by himself.

Percy isn't "more autistic" than Renee, and Renee isn't "more autistic" than Percy. Both of them are just autistic.

Thinking Differences

Autistic people think differently than non-autistic people.

Think about when you brush your teeth. Your brain thinks about a lot when you brush your teeth.

You think about how to hold the toothbrush, how to put it in your mouth, and how long you should brush your teeth. Autism can change how you think about all of those things.

Special Interests

Many autistic people have very strong interests, which we call **special interests**.

For example, some autistic people have a special interest in trains. They think about trains a lot, and know a lot more about trains than other people. They want to spend most of their time thinking about trains.

There are all kinds of special interests. It might be something big, like science, or it might be something smaller, like a favorite band.

Sometimes, special interests only last a little while. You might only have a special interest for a week. Other times, you could have one for a few months or years. Some special interests stay with us our whole lives.

There might be times when you have no special interests, and there might be times when you have a lot of special interests. All of this is normal.

Special interests are good, because they make us happy! We can use our special interests to help people, and they can be useful in our jobs. Special interests are really important to most autistic people.

Executive Functioning

Executive functioning is a group of skills that help people stay on track.

Staying on track means things like:

- ○ Following a plan
- ○ Starting something new
- ○ Stopping what you are doing
- ○ Remembering what to do next
- ○ Moving on to the next thing

For example:

> Emily works as a waiter at a restaurant, and she is in charge of a few things. First, she has to help set up the restaurant. Then, people come to the restaurant, and she has to help customers order food. When people are done eating, she has to clean up.
>
> Emily uses a lot of executive functioning. She has to start a lot of things, stop them when she's done, and plan and remember what to do next.

Autistic people can have a hard time with executive functioning. It may be hard to make a plan for what to do, start something new, or stop what you're doing. It may be hard to remember what you want to do.

Executive functioning problems can feel like being lazy, but having problems with executive functioning is not being lazy. You are not lazy. People with executive functioning problems want to do something, but we might not be able to without help.

Executive functioning problems can feel like riding a stubborn horse. No matter what you want, the horse ignores you! If you want the horse to run forward, it stays still. If you want the horse to stop, it keeps running. If you want the horse to change directions, it keeps going forward. In this example, the horse is your brain and body. You might want to do something, but you just can't do it.

Executive functioning is hard for us. We might need extra support, and that's okay! It's okay to need help.

Meltdowns and shutdowns

Meltdowns are when an autistic person can't control our feelings, and they happen when someone gets too stressed. People having meltdowns might scream or cry, run away, or lose control of our body.

Shutdowns can also happen when someone gets too stressed. A shutdown is when someone stops being able to do anything. We might not be able to talk or move.

Meltdowns and shutdowns feel scary to autistic people, and they can look scary to other people.

But they don't happen on purpose, and they are not the same thing as tantrums. Autistic people can't control when we have a meltdown or shutdown.

Other thinking differences

There are lots of ways autistic people think differently. Here are a few:

Autistic people can notice small things that other people don't notice. We can notice small mistakes that other people don't see, like typos. We can pay a lot of attention to things other people don't think are important. We can have very good memories for facts, like facts about our special interests.

Many autistic people like routine. We might like things to be the same every day, or to eat the same foods every day. It helps us to know what will happen each day.

Change can be scary for us, since things being the same helps us stay calm. Knowing what's coming helps us make sense of our lives.

Autistic people sometimes think in black and white. For example, things are either good or bad, we either like or dislike people, or we either can or can't do something. We can sometimes think in-between, but it can be hard. Black and white thinking can be a good thing. For example, we know when something is right or wrong, and we can help people do the right thing.

Autistic people learn things differently. We might learn things in a different order, like learning "hard" things before "easy" things. We might be great at one thing and bad at another thing. We might not get something, and then suddenly get it weeks later. We might need to learn some things very slowly, and other things very fast, or we might need to learn something more than once. Because we learn things differently, we can solve problems that other people can't!

Sensory Processing Differences

Processing is how your brain thinks about and reacts to things. **Sensory processing** is a type of processing, which is how you think about and understand your senses.

For example, if you look at a sock, you might notice certain things about it, like what color and size it is. If you touch it, you'll feel the fabric, and if you smell it, you'll notice other things. It might smell like sweat or laundry sheets. That's all sensory processing! Autism changes sensory processing in a lot of ways.

We have five major senses:

- **Vision:** Vision uses our eyes, and it's how we look at things. We can see color, lightness and darkness, shape, and texture. We can see how close or far something is, or what type of thing it is.

- **Touch:** Touch uses our hands or skin, and it's how we feel things. We can feel the texture of something, and tell how big or small it is. We can feel what shape it is, and how heavy or light something is. We can tell if food is soft or hard.

- **Hearing:** Hearing uses our ears, and it's how we listen to things. We can hear sounds and tell how loud or quiet they are, and if a sound is close or far away. We can tell what kind of thing might be making a noise, and tell noises apart from each other.

- **Smell:** Smell uses our nose, and it's how we figure out what something smells like. We can tell if something is stinky or smells good. We can tell different foods apart from each other.

- **Taste:** Taste uses our tongue, and it's how we tell the flavor of something. We can taste food and decide if we like it or not. We can taste if something is sour, sweet, spicy, or salty, and if food is hot or cold.

There are other senses too, such as:

- **Pressure:** Pressure is how we tell when things are touching us. It also helps you know how heavy things are.

- **Hunger and thirst:** Hunger is how we tell if we have had enough food to eat. Thirst lets us know if we have had enough to drink.

- **Pain:** Pain is how we tell if we are hurt or sick. More pain usually means you are more hurt or sick.

- **Temperature:** Temperature is how hot or cold something is.

- **Balance:** Balance is how we stay standing up and walk straight.

We use sensory processing to understand what we see, touch, hear, smell and taste.

Each person processes their senses a little differently, but autistic people process our senses a LOT differently. For example, loud noises might bother us, or we might like dim lights more than bright lights. We might like the texture of one food and hate the texture of a different food.

You might sense something a lot or only a little. If one of your senses is too strong, you might not be able to pay attention to anything else. If one of your senses is too weak, might not notice the sense at all.

Many autistic people have senses that are too strong or weak. Tags on clothing might really bother us, or we might get too hot even if the temperature isn't very high. We might not feel pain if we get hurt, or we might not notice a really bad smell.

Sometimes, our senses might feel like too much, which is called **sensory overload**. Sensory overload can make us angry or upset, or even cause a meltdown or a shutdown.

Autistic people can notice things that other people miss. We might love the fabric of a soft shirt, or love strong-tasting foods.

Our senses might change day to day. The tag on our shirt might bother us on one day, but tomorrow, it might be okay. It's okay to feel things differently. There is no right or wrong way to process things.

Stimming

Stimming is moving in the same way over and over again. People stim for all sorts of reasons. We stim to help balance out our senses, show how we feel, or focus on things. Stimming can help us feel better, and it's also a great way to have fun.

There are a lot of ways to stim, and here are a few examples:

- Rocking back and forth
- Flapping your hands
- Rubbing soft things on your face or body
- Humming, grunting, mumbling, moaning, or singing

- Spinning things or holding objects in front of your eyes

Almost anything can be a stim! People stim in different ways. One person might like rocking back and forth, while another person might like spinning around instead.

Non-autistic people stim too! For example, clicking a pen or tapping your foot is stimming. Everyone stims, but autistic people stim more than other people. Sometimes, we choose to stim because it helps us, and other times, we can't control how or when we stim.

Sometimes non-autistic people say that stims are too distracting. They say that if you stim, you shouldn't get to be around other people. These people are wrong! We should get to do the same things as other people. It doesn't matter what our body is doing.

Autistic people with all kinds of jobs stim. Autistic people stim at home, at school, on the street, and in movie theaters. Autistic people have stimmed in the White House! No one should ever force you to stop stimming.

Motor Differences

Autistic people have different motor skills than non-autistic people. **Motor skills** are how people control the way their body moves. Your body moves in big and small ways. Some big ways are running or swimming, and some small ways are writing or tying your shoes. Motor skills are also a part of talking, since moving your mouth to make sounds is a motor skill.

Not every autistic person has big differences in motor skills. Many autistic people have small motor differences, and we might not realize we have them! Motor differences can make someone have messy handwriting, be clumsy, or walk differently than other people.

Autistic people can have different kinds of motor problems, like:

- Planning how you are going to move

- Having trouble starting or stopping when you move

- Bumping into things, tripping, or dropping things

Here's an example:

> Alexis is autistic. She is sitting on the couch, and wants to get up and eat cereal. There are many things that might be hard for her. First, she has to stand up, then she has to walk to the kitchen. After that, she has to get the cereal, a bowl, and a spoon, and pour the cereal into the bowl.
>
> Alexis has to think about all the steps before she can do them. She has trouble remembering what the steps are, and may not know what order they go in. She may have a hard time getting up from the couch. Once she starts moving, she may have a hard time stopping at the kitchen. She may drop the cereal or the bowl when she tries to get them.

There are lots of people like Alexis. Maybe you also have trouble with these things.

Talking

Many autistic people have motor differences that change how we talk. We use our muscles to talk, but our muscles don't always work the way we want them to. This can make talking hard.

We have to figure out what we want to say, and how to make sounds with our mouth. We might not always know how, and even if we do, we might not be able to.

Some of us might hear differently, which can make it hard to figure out the right sounds to use. Figuring out the words we want can be hard, too. We might need to plan out what we want to say, and it can take us a while. People aren't always patient with us, and we might not be able to find the words we want at all!

Starting or stopping talking can be hard, since our muscles might not work when we need them to. We can't always talk when we want to, and we can't always stop talking when we want to.

All of this can change how autistic people talk. For example, many autistic people can't control our voices. We may talk too loud or too soft, or mumble or sound like we're singing when we talk.

Some people can't talk some or all of the time. Sometimes, this is because motor skills make it hard, but there might be other reasons. Lots of people don't think in words, or we might have anxiety that makes talking hard. There are all sorts of reasons.

People who don't talk are **non-speaking**. Here are a few examples of what a non-speaking person might look like:

- A person who has not talked at all in their whole life

- A person who talked as a kid but can't anymore

- A person who can talk sometimes, but writes words instead of talking

These are only some examples of what being non-speaking might look like! Some people are non-speaking as kids, but learn to talk later in life. Some people talk sometimes and not other times.

We don't know exactly how many autistic people are non-speaking. Right now, we think that about 1 out of 3 autistic people are non-speaking.

Communication Differences

Communication is how we show others what we want and need. All autistic people communicate, but we communicate in different ways than non-autistic people. Some of us use words, while others don't. Some of us talk with our mouths, while others are non-speaking.

Autistic people communicate in different ways. If we use words, we might use them differently. We might have a different sense of humor, or we might not like making small talk.

We understand things differently! For example, we might not understand if someone is joking, or we might understand pictures better than words.

Here are more ways autistic people communicate:

Echolalia

Echolalia means repeating things that you have heard before. For example, you might repeat lines from your favorite movie out loud.

Non-autistic people also say things from movies, books, or TV shows, but autistic people use echolalia a lot more. Autistic people use echolalia to communicate, and we use it when making new sentences is hard.

There are different kinds of echolalia. Some autistic people remember sentences that we hear, then we use them later. Here's an example:

> Bob's sister doesn't want to do the dishes, so she says "the dishwasher is broken." Later, Bob doesn't want to do his homework. He remembers what his sister said, so he says, "the dishwasher is broken." Bob is using echolalia. He is saying that he doesn't want to do something, but he isn't actually talking about the dishwasher. This can be hard for non-autistic people to understand.

Sometimes, we use echolalia in other ways. We can learn how to put together parts of different sentences.

For example:

> Bob wants to stay home, but his mom wants to go out. Bob's mom says "get in the car." Bob remembers when his sister said "the dishwasher is broken.", so he puts the sentences together. He says "the car is broken." He is saying that he wants to stay home.

Another kind of echolalia happens faster. We might repeat things right after we hear them.

Sometimes, this can be a problem.

For example:

> Juanita's mom says, "Do you want juice or water?" Juanita says "or water", but Juanita actually wanted juice. She could only say the last thing she heard, so she said "water" when she didn't mean to.

Some autistic people also use echolalia to stim. We like the way certain things sound, so we say them over and over again. Sometimes, we might not be able to stop saying something. We might not want you to pay attention to us when this happens. If you think this is happening, just ask us.

Scripting

Scripting is when people plan ahead of time what they want to say. For example, you might use a script to talk to your doctor. Scripts might be things you heard before, things you made up, or a combination of both.

Almost everyone uses scripts sometimes. Non-autistic people might script in small talk. They might say the same thing every time, like "How are you?", or they might script to plan ahead for things like job interviews. But autistic people script a lot more, and our scripts can be more thought-out than non-autistic people's scripts.

Augmentative and Alternative Communication (AAC)

AAC means using something other than talking to communicate. Sometimes, AAC adds onto talking, and other times, people use AAC instead of talking. Both speaking and non-speaking autistic people use AAC. Some people use AAC all of the time, and others only use it sometimes.

There are lots of different kinds of AAC, like:

- Typing on a computer
- Pushing buttons on an iPad
- Pointing to letters or pictures on a board
- Using sign language

Just because we can't talk, doesn't mean we can't communicate. Autistic people communicate in all sorts of ways! No matter how we communicate, we should be listened to. Talking isn't better than other kinds of communication.

Socializing Differences

Autism also changes how we socialize. **Socializing** means how we get along with other people.

Part of socializing is making friends. A big part of socializing is how other people feel about us.

Some people say that autism makes you bad at socializing, but these people are wrong! Autism means that we socialize *differently*, and socializing differently is okay.

Some people say the biggest part of autism is that we are bad at socializing. This is because socializing is very important to non-autistic people. When someone socializes differently, they notice right away. But socializing is just one part of autism. Other things, like how we think, feel, and move, are also important.

Here are some ways socializing can be different for autistic people.

Empathy

People use the word empathy to mean a lot of different things. Usually, **empathy** means caring how other people feel.

Some people say that autistic people don't have empathy, but they are wrong! We care a lot about how other people feel. Some autistic people can't stop caring, even when we don't want to.

We might feel really bad if we throw a toy away, since it can feel like we're hurting the toy's feelings. If we see someone who is hurt or embarrassed, we might feel the same way.

Guessing how other people feel

Everyone shows how they feel differently. No one can really know how someone else feels, but we can guess. Some people also call this "empathy."

Guessing how others feel is a big part of how most people socialize. You change how you act around someone when you guess how they feel. If you guess that someone is sad, you might try to cheer them up. If you guess they are angry, you might leave them alone.

No one is perfect at guessing, but most non-autistic people are pretty good at it. For most autistic people, it is very hard to guess how someone feels. We might need people to tell us how they feel. Non-autistic people are usually good at guessing feelings, but they are usually *bad* at guessing how autistic people feel. Autistic people might show our feelings in different ways, and we also think differently. That's why it can be harder for non-autistic people to guess our feelings.

Rules nobody says

There are a lot of rules for socializing. For example:

- When you see someone, ask them how they're doing.

- When someone asks you how you're doing, say you're doing well.

- Talk quietly indoors.

- Wear fancy clothes to fancy events.

- Only talk about things you like for a little bit.

- Don't interrupt people.

Many of these rules are not written down or said out loud. People just expect us to know them. This can be really hard for autistic people. How can we know a rule if no one tells us?

Non-autistic people don't have to think about the rules, since they just know how to follow them. But we have to think about the rules and how to follow them. We might not be able to follow them.

For example:

> Sonya is in the library, and the rule is to be quiet in the library. But Sonya can't be quiet, since her mouth makes noises even when she wants to be quiet. Sonya cares about the rule, and thinks about the rule a lot. But she can't follow the rule.

The rules also change sometimes. It depends on where you are and what's happening. It is hard for autistic people to know when the rules change.

For example:

> Jane is autistic. She feels sick, so she goes to the doctor. The doctor asks "How are you?" Jane says "I feel sick. My head hurts and my nose is runny." It is good that Jane says this to the doctor, because this helps the doctor know what to do.
>
> After going to the doctor, Jane goes to a restaurant. The waiter says "How are you?" Jane says "I feel sick. My head hurts and my nose is runny." The waiter is just being polite, and does not want to know how Jane is actually feeling. Jane could have just said "I am good."

A lot of autistic people spend a lot of time trying to figure out the rules. We might come up with our own ways to understand the rules, or come up with our own rules. This is a lot of work.

Thinking for ourselves

Autistic people are good at thinking for ourselves.

Lots of people have to deal with **peer pressure**, which is when people around you tell you to do something. You might do that thing even if you don't want to, because you want people to like you. For example, you might watch a movie you hate because your friends want to see it.

Non-autistic people have a hard time saying no to peer pressure. They get very upset if they think people will not like them. Autistic people can also have a hard time with peer pressure, but it is easier for us to think for ourselves. We might not feel peer pressure as much.

Because we think for ourselves, we sometimes ignore rules. For example, if we are at a party that is too loud, we might leave, even though we know the normal rule is to stay.

Non-autistic people usually agree with each other about what is important, but autistic people might not see things the same way.

For example:

> James is autistic. He has a friend named Anne. Anne says a raccoon got into her house and messed up her room. Anne's other friends focus on helping Anne clean up her room. James agrees that Anne needs help cleaning up her room, but he thinks it's important to make sure the raccoon is okay first. Anne's other friends don't agree with James. James isn't doing anything wrong, and neither are Anne's friends. They just have different ideas.

Eye Contact

Many autistic people don't make eye contact. Making eye contact can hurt us or make it hard to pay attention. It can be hard to listen to what someone says and look at their eyes at the same time. So we don't look at their eyes.

Non-autistic people can tell someone's feelings by looking at their eyes. They also use eye contact to share their own feelings. That's why eye contact is so important to them. Autistic people have different ways of sharing our feelings, and we usually don't use eye contact to do that. For example, we might just say how we are feeling.

Sometimes, some autistic people seem to make eye contact. We might learn how to pretend to make eye contact, like looking at someone's nose instead of their eyes. Or we might look in someone's eyes even though we don't like to. Some autistic people don't mind making eye contact, but most of us do.

Nonverbal communication

Eye contact is one kind of nonverbal communication. **Nonverbal communication** is communication that doesn't use language, like:

- Body language

- Facial expressions

- Tone of voice

People use nonverbal communication all the time, and you cannot stop yourself from using it. Any time someone can see you, they can see your nonverbal communication.

Non-autistic people know how to figure out what nonverbal communication usually means. They don't have to think about it very much. For example, when someone has their arms crossed, they know that person is angry. When someone is tapping their foot, they know the person is impatient. When someone smiles in a certain way, they know the person is happy.

But autistic people can have different nonverbal communication than non-autistic people. We might cross our arms because we need to feel pressure, or we might tap our feet because we are stimming. This can confuse non-autistic people.

Nonverbal communication isn't just about what you do. It's also about what other people think. People can guess how someone feels from their nonverbal communication, but people can make mistakes when they guess.

It can be extra hard for autistic people to guess or to understand nonverbal communication.

For example:

Bob is autistic, and he sees his friend Sally smiling. Bob thinks that Sally is happy because she is smiling, but Sally is actually angry. Sometimes people smile when they're angry. Bob doesn't understand that Sally is angry, so he tries to talk to Sally about happy things. This just makes Sally more angry.

Nonverbal communication has a lot of pieces. You have to use your voice, face and body to communicate to someone. That person is also communicating back to you with their voice, face and body. You also have to figure out what they are communicating. All of this happens at the same time, and it can be hard to deal with it all at once.

Autistic people might try to communicate with just our words instead. We make sure people can understand what we say, and that we understand what other people say. This works if the people we talk to can also just focus on words, but non-autistic people have a hard time doing that.

Putting it all together

Autistic people socialize differently than non-autistic people. We might like to text instead of talking on the phone. We might not like being around large groups of people, or to have conversations with confusing rules.

Other parts of autism also affect how we socialize. We may have trouble with loud noises, so we might not go to parties that are very loud. Moving can be hard, so we might not be able to go up to someone and start talking.

There are a lot of reasons why autistic people socialize differently. We should be able to do what works for us.

Daily Living

Autism changes how we get around in the world. It changes how we think, how we feel, and how we communicate.

A lot of autistic people need help in our daily lives. We can have a hard time with some things, like moving our bodies. We might have a hard time talking to people, or doing things that have a lot of steps. For example, cooking can be very hard for us, since it takes a lot of time and has a lot of steps.

But people have to do things like cooking every day. It takes more energy for autistic people to do these things. We may not be able to do everything we need to every day, or we may not be able to do some of these things at all.

For example:

> Cass is autistic. They have work today, and go to a long work meeting. When they get home, they don't have the energy to cook. They can't figure out the steps to cook, but they need to eat. They can order food instead, or they can get someone to help them cook.
>
> Roland is autistic. He can't cook because figuring out all the steps is too hard for him. He lives with a support person, who cooks for him. Roland helps around the house in other ways.

It is normal to need help in your daily life. All people, autistic or not, need help to live. Think about yourself and the people you know.

Let's say someone can drive a car, and they don't need help driving. But, can they fix their car by themselves? Did they build the car by themselves? Did they make all the parts for the car by themselves? Did they build all the roads the car drives on by themselves? You might know someone who does one or two of these things, but no one can do all these things on their own. We all need help.

Autistic people might need more help, so we might go about our daily lives in a different way.

Here are a few examples:

- Someone who needs help being safe might live with a support person.

- Someone who has a hard time listening at school might have someone take notes for them.

- Someone who has a hard time shopping might get their groceries delivered instead.

- Someone who has a hard time remembering what to do might have a job coach at work.

It is okay to need help. You should always get the help you need, and there is nothing wrong with asking for help.

Autistic people have lots of things we're good at, and lots of things we need help with. We are not like non-autistic people, and that's okay. We shouldn't have to act like non-autistic people, and non-autistic people should respect us as we are.

Only autistic people can say what autism means to us, and decide how other people can help us.

Chapter Two Resources

You can find the links to these resources at
autismacceptance.com/book/chapter-2-resources

- Everyone Communicates - the AAC Resource

- In My Language - by Mel Baggs

- Why We Should Stop Stim Suppression - by Cassandra Crosman

Who Can Be Autistic?

The way people talk about autism has changed a lot.

We used to call autism a lot of different things. Some people still use these words, like:

- Autism Spectrum Disorder (ASD)

- Autistic Disorder

- Asperger's Syndrome

- Childhood Disintegrative Disorder

- Pervasive Developmental Disability Not Otherwise Specialized (PDD-NOS)

- Atypical Autism

Today, we mostly just call it autism.

People with other disabilities can also be autistic, and autistic people can have more than one disability. Sometimes, these other disabilities are part of being autistic, and other times, they aren't part of being autistic. Autism is a developmental disability, and many people with developmental disabilities have more than one disability. That's normal.

Here are some other disabilities autistic people sometimes have:

Learning disabilities (called "learning difficulties" in the United Kingdom):

- Dyslexia

- Dyspraxia

- Dysgraphia

- Dyscalculia

- Nonverbal Learning Disability

Mental health disabilities:

- Depression

- Anxiety

- Bipolar disorder

- PTSD

- Schizophrenia

- Eating Disorders

- OCD

- Tourette's Syndrome

Disabilities that affect your body:

- Connective tissue disorders, like Ehlers-Danlos syndrome and Marfan syndrome
- Sleep disorders, like insomnia or sleep apnea
- Digestion disorders, like GERD and peptic ulcer disease
- Epilepsy
- Tuberous Sclerosis

Other developmental disabilities:

- Intellectual disabilities (called "learning disabilities" in the United Kingdom)
- ADHD
- Rett's Syndrome
- Angelman's Syndrome
- Down Syndrome
- Cerebral Palsy

Some disabilities happen more in autistic people. Sometimes, people say that means autism is a bad thing, but that doesn't make sense.

Think of it like this:

People with red hair sunburn more easily. Sunburns hurt and can cause skin cancer, but we don't say that red hair is bad. We don't try to cure red hair, or tell people with red hair to dye their hair. That wouldn't help with their sunburns. Instead, we make sure people wear sunblock.

It's the same with autism. Autistic people should get more support for all of our disabilities. We don't need people to try and fix us!

Sometimes, autistic people don't get an autism diagnosis, and we might get diagnosed with other disabilities instead. Sometimes, we also have these disabilities, but other times, doctors are just confused. They might not realize we are autistic.

Women and people of color get the wrong diagnosis the most, and get diagnosed with other disabilities instead.

Some of these other disabilities are:

- Deafness

- Schizophrenia

- Borderline Personality Disorder

- Avoidant Personality Disorder

- Schizotypal Personality Disorder

- Oppositional Defiant Disorder

- Social (Pragmatic) Communication Disorder

- Nonverbal Learning Disorder

- Sensory Processing Disorder

- Depression

- Bipolar Disorder

- Anxiety

- Obsessive-compulsive disorder (OCD)

- Attention Deficit Hyperactivity Disorder (ADHD)

- Intellectual Disability

Autistic people can have disabilities besides autism. But some doctors don't know a lot about autism, and might say we have these disabilities *instead* of autism. Doctors can be wrong.

Anyone can be autistic. Girls, women, transgender people, and non-binary people can be autistic. People of color can be autistic. Teenagers, adults, and older people can be autistic. People with other disabilities can also be autistic.

Girls and women can be autistic!

Girls and women get diagnosed with autism less than boys. Lots of people think of autism as a "boys' thing", so girls might get diagnosed with other disabilities instead. They might be told they're just shy or mean, but that is wrong! Girls can be autistic, too.

Autistic girls might not always look like autistic boys, since girls and boys might act differently. Girls might feel more pressure to fit in than boys do, and this can make it harder to tell if girls are autistic.

Studies about autism mostly focus on autistic boys. This means that we know very little about autistic girls, which makes it even harder for girls to get diagnosed.

Transgender and non-binary people can be autistic!

There are lots of different genders, but some people think there are only 2. When people are born, the doctor usually says "It's a boy!" or "It's a girl!". The doctor says this based on what someone's body looks like, but sometimes the doctor is wrong. You don't have to be a boy or girl just because of what your body looks like.

Sometimes, a person who was told she was a boy is actually a girl. **Transgender** means your gender is different than people thought when you were born. **Cisgender** means your gender is the same as people thought when you were born.

For example:

> Billy is transgender. When Billy was born, everyone thought he was a girl, but Billy knew he was a boy. Billy told people that he was a boy, and now, he lives his life as a man.

There are lots of different genders. Sometimes, a person is not a boy or a girl. Sometimes, a person does not have a gender, or feels like different genders at different times. **Non-binary** means that someone isn't just a boy or a girl.

A lot of autistic people are transgender or non-binary, and we do not know why this happens.

That is okay! It is okay to be autistic, transgender or non-binary, or both!

Some people say that autistic people cannot understand ourselves. They might just say that we are confused about our gender, but they are wrong! Autistic people get to decide what our genders are, no matter what.

People of color can be autistic!

People of color are people who are not white. Some examples of people of color are Black people, Asian people, and Latinx people. Anyone who isn't white is a person of color.

White people get diagnosed with autism more than people of color, but people of color are just as likely to be autistic. Doctors aren't very good at diagnosing autistic people of color. Racism can make it harder for autistic people of color to get diagnosed. They might get diagnosed with a different disability instead.

We need to work hard to support autistic people of color. Everyone should be able to find out if they are autistic.

Teenagers, adults, and older people can be autistic!

Anyone can be autistic, regardless of how old you are. You can't "grow out" of autism!

Remember: autism is a developmental disability, so if a person is autistic, they never stop being autistic. This means that people of all ages can be autistic.

Sometimes, people get diagnosed with autism when they are an adult. They didn't have a chance to get diagnosed as a kid, or their doctor made a mistake. That doesn't mean someone wasn't autistic as a kid. They were still autistic their whole life, even before they got a diagnosis.

Any type of person can be autistic. Autistic people are all kinds of people!

Chapter Three Resources

You can find the links to these resources at
autismacceptance.com/book/chapter-3-resources

- Autism Self-Diagnosis is not Special Snowflake Syndrome - by Sara Luterman

- Autistic Women & Nonbinary Network

- Adult Misdiagnosis – The Default Path to an Autistic Identity - by Autistic Science Lady

- Why It's So Difficult to Diagnose Autism in Girls - by Somer Bishop

- Autism's Race Problem - by Pacific Standard

Autism Facts

Many people get confused about autism, and there's a lot of wrong information about autism out there. In this chapter, we will talk about some wrong ideas people have about autism, and show you how autism actually works.

1. Vaccines do not cause autism

Vaccines are shots you get to help you not get sick. For example, the flu shot is a vaccine that keeps you from getting sick with the flu.

In 1997, a scientist named Andrew Wakefield lied and said that vaccines caused autism. Lots of scientists proved him wrong, and showed that autism is not caused by vaccines. But some people still believe vaccines cause autism. They don't give their kids vaccines since they think it is better for their kids to get sick than to be autistic. It hurts autistic people to hear that other people are so scared of us.

It is safe to get vaccines, and vaccines keep people from getting sick. If people weren't so scared of autism, they would be calm about vaccines. That would be better for everyone.

We don't always know what makes people autistic, but we do know that autism is mostly genetic. That means you get it before you are born, and it comes from your family. Autistic people sometimes have a lot of autistic family members.

In the end, what causes autism doesn't matter very much. What matters is supporting autistic people. We should be able to have good lives no matter what.

---

2. Autism is not a disease. You can't cure autism.

A disease is something that makes you sick. Diseases can really hurt or even kill people. When someone has a disease, they need to see a doctor to "get better" from their disease.

Autism is not a disease. Autism is just how our brain works. Autism doesn't make you sick, and you can't die from autism. Doctors can't stop us from being autistic, and we don't "get better" by not being autistic. We are autistic our whole lives, and that is just how we are!

People usually want a cure for diseases, but most autistic people don't want a cure for autism.

The goal of a cure is to "fix" something, and autistic people don't need to be fixed.

Some people don't care what we want. They want a cure for autism, and they spend a lot of time and money looking for it. This is bad for autistic people. People should spend time and money helping us live good lives.

---

3. There is no "normal" person inside an autistic person.

Some people talk about autism like it is not part of who we are. They think there is secretly a "normal" person inside us, and say autism keeps us from being normal.

They want to get rid of our autism so we can be normal, but you can't make us normal by getting rid of our autism. Autistic people are autistic all the way through. There is no normal person trapped inside an autistic person. Autism is just part of who we are. We are autistic, and that's good.

---

4. Autistic people have always been in the world.

People say that there are more autistic people now than there used to be, but this is not true. Doctors are just getting better at finding us.

In the year 2000, doctors said that about 1 in 150 people were autistic. Right now, they think 1 in 59 people are autistic. This isn't because more autistic people are being born. It's because doctors are getting better.

Doctors still aren't perfect. They miss some autistic people, like girls and people of color. Doctors are trying to get better at figuring out who is autistic. That means the number of diagnosed autistic people might keep going up. This is a good thing, since it means more autistic people can get the help we need.

5. It's okay to be autistic! Autism is not sad.

Autism is just a way some brains work. Autistic people have things that are hard for us, like everyone else does. We also have strengths! There are things about autism that make life harder, but that does not mean that autism is sad.

A lot of the things that are hard for autistic people aren't hard because of autism. They are hard because of other people. For example, people might treat us badly because we are autistic. They might not understand autism, and they might try to keep us separate from non-autistic people. None of this means that autism is bad. It means that other people are being unfair. We need to make the world a better place for autistic people.

6. Autistic adults are adults. That means that we have the minds of adults.

Some people talk about something called "mental age". People use mental age when they talk about developmental disabilities. Adults with developmental disabilities need help with a lot of things. Some of those are things that most kids can do by themselves, so people say that in our minds, we are like kids.

Some autistic people have interests that usually only kids have. We might also talk like kids do, or play in the same ways that kids play. People might say we are like kids, but these people are wrong.

For example:

Beth is 36 and has an intellectual disability. She does not know left from right, and she really likes Blue's Clues. A doctor says that Beth is like a 5-year-old, and says she is "mentally 5." This doesn't make sense, since Beth has been alive for 36 years. Her brain is not like a 5-year-old's brain, and it is rude to say that she is like a child.

Being a kid isn't about what you can and can't do, or about how you talk or play. Neither is being an adult. You learn and grow every year you are alive. People are the age they are, and mental ages aren't real. Autistic adults don't have the minds of kids. We have the minds of autistic adults, and autistic adults with intellectual disabilities are still adults.

Autistic people can do anything that any other adult can do. Autistic people can have sex, get married, have kids, make our own choices, and live our lives. We might do things differently than non-autistic people, and we might need more help. But we are still adults.

---

7. Autistic people are autistic our whole lives.

Autistic people are born autistic. But since all babies look the same, we don't know a lot about how babies will turn out until they get older. We usually don't know if a baby is autistic until they are a toddler. That doesn't mean the baby became autistic when they became a toddler. They were autistic before, but people could not tell.

Autistic people grow up to be adults. We don't stop being autistic, and you can't grow out of autism. If you are autistic now, you have been autistic since you were born, and you will be autistic when you die. Adults and kids look and act different. This is true for everyone. Autistic adults look and act differently than autistic kids. We learn new skills, get new hobbies, and make new friends. Things that were hard when we were kids might get easier.

Most movies, books, and stories focus on autistic kids, so many people do not think there are autistic adults. But there are autistic adults! We just look different.

Some autistic people get taught to pretend they aren't autistic. People might punish us if we act autistic, but we are still autistic inside. Pretending not to be autistic is really hard, and it hurts us.

We might get better at pretending as we become adults. People might see us and think we are not autistic, but that's not true. We are still autistic—we're just pretending not to be, and that hurts us.

Autistic kids grow up into autistic adults. We shouldn't have to pretend that we are not autistic. People should know autistic adults exist.

8. Most autistic people talk. All autistic people communicate.

Some people think that autistic people can't talk, but these people are wrong. Most autistic people can talk. Some autistic people talked when we were little kids, and some of us took longer to learn how to talk. Some of us can talk, but it is hard. It's true that some autistic people can't talk at all, and that's okay! There are lots of different ways to communicate, and all autistic people communicate. We can still communicate, regardless of whether we can talk or not.

9. Autism and intellectual disability are not the same thing.

Autism and intellectual disability have some parts that are the same, but they are different disabilities. You can have both, or only one, or neither.

Intellectual disabilities affect how you learn and think. People with intellectual disabilities might learn more slowly, and they might need more help with everyday life. People with intellectual disabilities do learn and think, just differently.

Some autistic people also have intellectual disabilities, but most autistic people don't. There are a lot of different ways to be autistic!

10. Don't assume things about non-speaking people.

Lots of people have wrong ideas about people who are non-speaking. People think that if someone is non-speaking, they have an intellectual disability, don't have anything to say, or don't care about other people.

All of these ideas are wrong. Non-speaking people don't talk, and that's the only thing different about them. Just because someone can't talk doesn't mean they have nothing to say. It doesn't mean they don't care about people, or that they have an intellectual disability.

You should help non-speaking people communicate in ways that work for them. If someone is non-speaking, try to understand them and get to know them. Don't assume things because you don't understand.

11. Autistic people know that everyone has thoughts.

Some scientists say that autistic people don't understand other people. They say we don't know that other people have thoughts, or that different people have different thoughts.

That is very silly. Autistic people know that other people have thoughts, and we have said this for a long time. In this book, we talk about what other people think a lot, and that shows that we know that other people have thoughts. Maybe reading this book would help scientists understand how *we* think.

12. Autistic people are in the same world as everyone else.

Some people say that autistic people are "in our own world." They think we don't notice things going on around us, or that we don't care about other people or other things.

This is wrong. Autistic people are in the same world as everyone else. We are right here, but we just see the world differently. Autism changes how we act with other people, but we are still part of the world.

Sometimes it might look like we are not paying attention or noticing things, but that could be for a lot of reasons. It doesn't mean we are "in our own world".

---

13. Not all autistic people are extra good at things.

Some autistic people are better than almost everyone else at certain things. For example, they might know the day of the week of any day in history. Maybe they can draw a city perfectly from memory, or they might be able to do very hard math in their heads.

Most autistic people are not this way. We are good at some things and bad at some things, but it is very rare to be the best at something.

---

14. People of all genders are autistic.

Right now, more boys and men get diagnosed with autism than girls and women. Boys are diagnosed with autism about 3 times as much as girls, but that doesn't mean that there are more autistic boys than autistic girls.

The tests doctors use to diagnose autism were made just by looking at boys. Doctors decided what autism means by looking at boys, so a lot of autistic women and girls get left out. They are autistic, but doctors don't notice.

Plus, autistic people are lots of different genders. There are more genders than just boys and girls, but nobody is counting people who aren't boys or girls.

Since we are missing so many people, the autism diagnosis numbers are wrong. We don't know what the real numbers are, but we do know that people of all genders can be autistic.

15. People of all races are autistic.

Anyone of any race can be autistic. Because of racism, white people get diagnosed with autism more than people of color. But people of color are autistic just as often as white people.

The tests doctors use to diagnose autism were made just by looking at white boys. Doctors decided what autism means by looking at white boys, and they didn't think about autistic people who aren't white boys. That's why people of color get diagnosed with autism a lot less. They are autistic, but doctors don't notice. Now, doctors are starting to notice more, but people of color still do not get diagnosed as often as white people.

Autistic kids of color might not get diagnosed with autism, or they might get diagnosed with other disabilities instead of autism. For example, they might get diagnosed with an intellectual disability, or a mental health disability. A lot of times, the diagnosis is wrong! Doctors have wrong ideas about people of color, so they diagnose people of color with other disabilities instead of autism. This isn't fair!

People of color should get the right diagnosis. Everyone should know that people of color can be autistic, and that people of color are part of the autistic community.

Chapter Four Resources

You can find the links to these resources at **autismacceptance.com/book/chapter-4-resources**

- Mental Age Theory Hurts People with Disabilities - by Ivanova Smith

- Left Brain Right Brain: Autism News, Science, and Opinion

- "Putting on My Best Normal": Social Camouflaging in Adults with Autism Spectrum Conditions

Autism and Disability

Autism is a disability. What does that mean?

This chapter talks about:

- What disability means

- The disability rights movement

- The neurodiversity movement

How can we think about disability?

Disability is a normal part of society. A **society** is a big group of communities. The United States is one example of a society.

Society is supposed to help everyone get what they need, but society doesn't always do that. Our society hurts people with disabilities, and says that disability is a problem. It says that people should try to cure disability, and that people should try and be less disabled.

People with disabilities are not the problem. Instead, society is the problem. Society needs to help people with disabilities, not hurt us. Society shouldn't try to change disabled people. We should work to make sure people with disabilities can get what we need.

Disability isn't as big of a deal if things are accessible. **Accessibility** means disabled people can easily use something, get around somewhere, and feel like we belong there.

For example:

Charlene is blind. She goes to a restaurant, but the restaurant does not have a menu in Braille. The restaurant is too crowded to get around easily. The waiter doesn't try to help Charlene, and people nearby talk about her disability while she eats. The restaurant is *not* accessible to blind people.

Charlene goes to a different restaurant. The restaurant has bumps on the floor to help Charlene find a seat. They have a menu in Braille, and the waiter also says he can read the menu to Charlene. People nearby make friendly conversation with Charlene, and they don't ask rude questions about her disability. This restaurant *is* accessible to blind people.

There are things about some disabilities that can be hard. For example, autism is a disability, and might make it harder for someone to talk or get dressed by themselves. Accessibility doesn't make disability go away, but it still helps a lot.

Disability is a part of life, and disabled people will always be a part of the world. Many disabled people will always need help to live our daily lives, and that is okay! Disability makes us different and interesting people. We need to talk less about fixing people and more about fixing the world!

What is ableism?

Treating people badly because of who they are is called **discrimination**. **Ableism** is discrimination against disabled people. Ableism doesn't always happen on purpose, but ableism happens all the time.

Some non-disabled people think it is bad to be disabled. They don't always say that with their words, but instead with their actions. They don't accept people with disabilities, and they don't try and make things accessible. They keep us out of schools, neighborhoods, and jobs where non-disabled people are. They might abuse or hurt us. These things are all ableism.

Autistic people deal with certain kinds of ableism.

Here are some kinds of ableism we deal with:

- It is ableism when people want to cure autism. It means that people want to get rid of us. They try and make us act less autistic, but they should accept us for who we are!

- It is also ableism when people say we aren't autistic. People might not give us help we need, or they might say we aren't "autistic enough" to need help.

- It is ableism to ignore non-speaking autistic people. People might say we can't communicate, or take away things that help us communicate. They might hurt us because they know we can't tell someone else about it.

Ableism means that some people don't think about our needs. Because of this, they don't help us live good lives.

Autistic people aren't the only people who deal with ableism. All disabled people deal with ableism. Wheelchair users get told they aren't "disabled enough" to need a wheelchair, and Deaf people may not get interpreters during job interviews. People might try and keep disabled people from getting health care we need.

Ableism has been around for a long time, and disabled people have been treated badly for a long time. If you have dealt with ableism, you are not alone.

We know that there is nothing wrong with being disabled. We can be proud of who we are. People with disabilities work together, and show others that we are proud. We have worked together for many years, and we made the disability rights movement. The **disability rights movement** is when disabled people fight back against ableism. We work to change society to be better for disabled people, and fight for our rights as people with disabilities.

Neurodiversity

Neurodiversity is the idea that humans have all kinds of brains. Every person has things they are good at and things they need help with, and there is no such thing as a "normal" brain. Some of us have brains that think differently because of a disability, and that's okay!

People are different in all sorts of ways.

We have different:

- Genders
- Ages
- Races
- Cultures
- Bodies
- Religions
- And more!

We also have different brains!

The Neurodiversity Movement

The **neurodiversity movement** says it is okay to be disabled, and it is okay if your brain is different from other people's. The neurodiversity movement is part of the disability rights movement.

It says a few different things, such as:

- People with all kinds of brains should be accepted in society.

- People shouldn't try to cure or get rid of disabilities like autism.

- Autistic people should be allowed to be autistic.

- We should work to make sure that everyone gets the help we need.

The neurodiversity movement is for more than just autistic people. It is for people with intellectual disabilities, mental health disabilities, and learning disabilities. It is for people who talk, and people who don't. It is for people who only need a little bit of help, and people who need a lot of help all the time. The neurodiversity movement is for *everyone*.

Many autistic people have intellectual disabilities. People with intellectual disabilities made the self-advocacy movement, and the neurodiversity movement wouldn't be here without their help.

Chapter Five Resources

You can find the links to these resources at
autismacceptance.com/book/chapter-5-resources

- 10 Principles of Disability Justice - Sins Invalid

- Video: Social Model Animation

- The Disability Gulag - by Harriet McBryde Johnson

- Video: It's Our Story

- Medical Model vs Social Model - by Kids as Self Advocates (KASA)

- Judy Heumann Fights for People with Disabilities - Drunk History

- Parallels in Time: A History of Developmental Disabilities

- Autistic Community and the Neurodiversity Movement - by Steven Kapp

Self-Advocacy and the Self-Advocacy Movement

Autistic people have been standing up for ourselves forever, in lots of different ways.

This is called "self-advocacy". **Self-advocacy** means standing up for yourself so you get what you need.

This chapter will talk about these things:

- What self-advocacy is
- Who can be a self-advocate
- What the self-advocacy movement is
- How to be a self-advocate

What is Self-Advocacy?

Self-advocacy means a lot of things. It means standing up for yourself, taking control over your own life, and fighting for your right to live how you want to live. We self-advocate in ways that are both big and small.

For example:

Milo is an autistic high school student. They live in the United States. Their school has meetings to talk about what Milo needs. Milo's teachers and parents go to these meetings, and so does Milo. They speak up if they want a new kind of help, or if they disagree with their teachers or parents. This is one kind of self-advocacy!

Self-advocacy doesn't always look like that, though. There is no one "right" way to be a self-advocate. Here are some other kinds of self-advocacy:

- Saying "No!"

- Asking for help

- Telling someone to leave you alone

- Deciding what you want to do today

- Talking to other people about your disability

Self-advocacy can be something that you do by yourself, or with other disabled people.

Self-advocacy isn't just speaking up for yourself. It can also mean speaking up for your whole community. The **self-advocacy movement** is when we all speak up together. The self-advocacy movement is part of the disability rights movement, where people with intellectual and developmental disabilities fight for our rights.

The Self-Advocacy Movement

In the 1960s, Swedish people with intellectual disabilities got together. They formed their own clubs, where they talked about how they wanted to be treated. Then, the clubs told the world how they wanted to be treated.

This idea spread to other countries! Disabled people got together, and told others what we wanted and needed. We wanted to live at home in our communities, and we wanted to go to school and work with everyone else.

The self-advocacy movement grew and grew. Disabled people started running disability groups.

We closed a lot of institutions, wrote books about being disabled, and made laws to help disabled people live better lives. We changed the world!

We still have a long way to go, since disabled people still get treated unfairly. We can't always choose where we live or what help we get. We don't always have the right to vote. We might not get to choose how we want to spend our money, or have control over who cares for us. But we are still fighting for our rights.

A motto of the self-advocacy movement is "Nothing About Us, Without Us!". Lots of people talk about us without letting us talk. We should always be part of the conversation, and be in charge of our lives.

Who can be a self-advocate?

Anyone can be a self-advocate! If you are autistic, you are already a self-advocate.

You don't need to change laws to self-advocate. You can start small. You can practice standing up for yourself, and talking about things that are important to you. That is self-advocacy.

No one is too disabled to be a self-advocate. To be a self-advocate, you only need 2 things. You need to know what you want, and you need a way to show people what you want. That's it!

For example:

> Juanita doesn't talk or write, and she needs a helper. If she likes something, she tells her helper by humming. If she doesn't like something, she bites her hands. The people around Juanita pay attention to what she likes and doesn't like. If she doesn't like a helper, her family fires them. Juanita is a self-advocate.

How Can I Self-Advocate?

All you need to practice self-advocacy is yourself. No one needs to tell you what to do, and you don't need to start at a certain time. It is up to you!

You might not be sure where to start. Here's what self-advocacy might look like for you:

Saying "No!"

You can tell others what you are okay with and not okay with. You can say "No" when someone does something you aren't okay with, or use other ways to show that something isn't okay.

For example, if someone tries to touch you, you can say "Don't touch me." or say "No!". You could also just move away from that person.

Sometimes, you'll be okay with something one day, then not be okay with it later. It is okay to change your mind, and to say "No!" even if you said "Yes" before. How you feel is important, and other people should respect your feelings.

Talk to other people about yourself.

You can tell them about your disability, what you're good at, and things you need help with.

Your wants and your needs matter. You might want to try a new hobby, stay up later at night, or study in a quiet place. You might need help with different parts of life, like getting a job or health care. Other people can help you meet your goals, and the more they know about you, the more they can help.

Getting help.

There is nothing wrong with asking for help. Your family and friends can help, or you can ask someone whose job is to help people. You can also get accommodations to help you. **Accommodations** are changes that make things easier for disabled people, and help us get the same things as non-disabled people. Accommodations can be used at school or work, or in public places like restaurants.

Accommodations can be useful for all sorts of things. Here are some examples of accommodations at school:

- Getting extra time on a test

- Having a note-taker

- Using AAC in class

Wanting or needing accommodations isn't bad—it is normal. Non-disabled people have their needs met in most places, but disabled people don't. That is why accommodations exist, so don't be afraid to use them.

Use the things that work for you.

It is normal for things to be hard sometimes, but there are ways to make things easier. You can make your own accommodations. There are lots of tools autistic people use to make our lives easier, like:

- Printing out schedules with pictures to plan out your day

- Having a friend come over once a week to help you clean up

- Setting up a phone or laptop to remind you to do things

You might feel pressured to communicate in certain ways. People might want you to talk out loud, or push you to talk faster. They might want you to talk in ways that they like. You should communicate however works best for you. You might find writing easier than talking, or find it easier to point to pictures or draw things. You should communicate in a way that you like. That's self-advocacy!

Remember: self-advocacy is for everyone, and you are already a self-advocate. You can use some of these ideas to practice self-advocacy. The more you practice, the easier it will get.

Even when you self-advocate, people might be jerks, not listen to you, or treat you badly. When you think something is wrong, it can help to know your rights.

Chapter Six Resources

You can find the links to these resources at
autismacceptance.com/book/chapter-6-resources

- Self-Advocacy Online

- The Meaning of Self-Advocacy - by Mel Baggs

- I'm Determined: Empowering Self-Determined Behavior

- From Ableist to Self Advocate - by Amy Sequenzia

- Self-Determination Tools

Know Your Rights

Everyone has rights, including you!

The word "rights" can mean two things. Sometimes, rights are things that the law gives you. These are called **legal rights**, and the government has to make sure you get these rights.

The second meaning of "rights" is "things that you *should* have." People might say you have the "right" to be happy, but the government doesn't have to make sure that you are happy.

This chapter of the book will explain what *legal* rights you have. We will talk about laws that protect people with disabilities. This chapter focuses on rights in the United States of America, but other countries have their own disability rights laws. You can learn more about those at the end of this chapter.

Americans with Disabilities Act

The Americans with Disabilities Act is also called the ADA. The **ADA** is a law that gives people with disabilities lots of different rights. People say it is the biggest disability rights law in the United States.

The ADA says that you have a right to accommodations. Some examples of accommodations from the ADA are:

- Getting captions on a TV show

- Menus in Braille

- Bringing your service dog to work

- An interpreter at the doctor's office

The ADA gives people with disabilities rights at work. The law says that your boss can't discriminate against disabled people. Your boss can't fire you or treat you differently because you have a disability. You can get accommodations at work because of the ADA.

The ADA also gives you rights in places run by the government, such as:

- Libraries

- The post office

- City hall

- Public transportation, like buses, trains, and subways

The ADA says you have the right to go inside any place run by the government, and to use any service run by the government.

If a business is open to everyone, the ADA says you have the right to go inside, and to do the same things as everyone else.

For example:

- If you go to a hairdresser, you have the right to get a haircut.
- If you go to the movies, you have a right to captions.
- If you go to a store, you have the right to go inside and buy things.
- If you go to a restaurant, you have the right to order food.

The ADA says you have the right to communicate in ways that work for you, and to understand what is going on. Phone calls, text messages, and video calls have to be accessible.

The ADA is a very important law that gives people with disabilities the same rights as everyone else.

The IDEA

IDEA is a law that gives rights to students with disabilities, and stands for "Individuals with Disabilities Education Act." IDEA is for schools that get money from the government.

Not every student with a disability gets rights from IDEA. Autistic students do get rights from IDEA, but to get these rights, you need a diagnosis.

IDEA says you have the right to:

- Get a diagnosis for your disability

- Go to school

- Go to school for free, like everyone else

- Learn things in school

- Learn the same things as everyone else

- Be in the same classroom as non-disabled students

- Get the help you need to learn

IDEA says you can get services to help you learn in school. Schools need to make a plan called an **IEP** for each student with a disability. IEP means Individualized Education Plan.

The IEP has to say:

- What you know how to do right now
- What you need to learn
- What your goals at school are for the next year
- How the school will know if you are learning
- The services the school will give you
- Accommodations the school will make for you

Some students don't end up in the same classrooms as everyone else, or take the same tests as everyone else. If these things happen, the IEP needs to say why.

When you turn 16, you also get a **transition plan.** It helps you figure out what you will do after high school, and how you'll meet your goals after high school. You have the transition plan until you are done with school.

Rehabilitation Act and Section 504 Rights

There is a law called the Rehabilitation Act, that is called the "Rehab Act" for short. The **Rehab Act** makes rules for programs the government pays for. **Section 504** is the part of the Rehab Act that talks about disability rights.

The Rehab Act says the government can't discriminate against people with disabilities. If the government pays for something, it has to work for people with disabilities. For example:

- Government websites have to be accessible.
- Government buildings have to be accessible.
- The government can't discriminate against people with disabilities for jobs.

Places the government gives money to can't discriminate either. For example, if the government hires a business, the business can't discriminate.

The government gives some schools money, which means those schools also have to follow the Rehab Act. The school can make **Section 504 Plans** for disabled students, that say what a student needs to be able to learn. For example, the student might need:

- An iPad
- A letterboard

- Large print
- Sign language
- A support person

Some students get Section 504 plans, while other students get IEPs. It depends on the school and the student.

Fair Housing Act

The **Fair Housing Act** is another disability rights law, that makes sure people with disabilities have housing rights. It is called the FHA for short. Here are a few rights you get from the FHA:

- If you want to rent an apartment, landlords can't say no because of your disability.

- If you want to buy a house, sellers can't say no because of your disability.

- Your landlord has to let you put a ramp at your apartment if you need one.

- If you have a service dog, your landlord has to let it live with you, even if dogs usually aren't allowed.

Olmstead

Olmstead v. L.C. was a big court case about living in the community. People just call it *"Olmstead"* for short.

In 1999, two women named Lois Curtis and Elaine Wilson were living in an institution. They wanted to live in the community instead of an institution. They said the ADA gave them the right to live in the community, and they went to the Supreme Court to fight for their rights. The **Supreme Court** has the final say on how laws work, and they said that Lois and Elaine were right.

Olmstead means that you have a right to live in the community. If the government says you can only get services in an institution, they are wrong. You can get services in the community.

But *Olmstead* is a court case, not a law. That means you have to go to court to get your *Olmstead* rights. Lots of people are still fighting for their *Olmstead* rights.

Supported Decision-Making

Most adults make their own legal decisions, but some people with disabilities have **guardians**. A guardian can make legal decisions for a person with disabilities. A judge chooses who will be the guardian for a disabled person, but it is usually a parent or family member. Guardians can make choices even if the person with a disability doesn't like it. This is wrong!

There is something people with disabilities can do instead of getting a guardian, called supported decision-making. **Supported decision-making** means you get help making decisions, but they are still your decisions. You can choose people called "supporters" to help you make decisions. Supporters do not make the choices for you. You still make your own decisions.

If you have a guardian, you might be able to do supported decision-making instead. Laws about supported decision making are different in every state. Your **Protection & Advocacy Agency (P&A)** can help you learn more. P&A's help people with disabilities fight for our rights, and make sure states follow disability laws. There is a P&A in every state.

Chapter Seven Resources

You can find the links to these resources at
autismacceptance.com/book/chapter-7-resources

- The Americans with Disabilities Act of 1990 - Car Autism Roadmap

- Job Accommodation Network

- Inclusive Schools Network

- Wrightslaw Special Education Law and Advocacy

- Olmstead Self-Assessment

- How to Make a Supported Decision-Making Agreement - ACLU

- National Disability Rights Network

- Information on the ADA

- International Disability Alliance

- International Disability Rights - Disability Rights Education & Defense Fund

Finding and Creating Autistic Community

Doctors say that around 1 in 59 people are autistic, but doctors still aren't good at diagnosis. Many people don't get diagnosed, so the number of autistic people is probably more than 1 in 59! There are millions of autistic people all over the world, and we have a lot of ways to find each other.

What Is Autistic Community?

Some people think autistic people can't have a community. They say autistic people are loners, or that we can't have friends. These people are wrong! Autistic people have communities, and autistic community is very important.

Autistic community can mean a lot of different things. It can mean:

- Autistic people hanging out together
- Autistic people helping each other solve problems
- Autistic people talking to each other online
- Autistic people fighting for our rights

Autistic community doesn't have to be all about autism. Autistic community can be autistic people just hanging out. We might talk about things we like, play video games together, or do other things we enjoy.

Autistic community helps us feel good about who we are. It is important to get a chance to be yourself, and when everyone is autistic, it can be easier to be yourself.

It is important to spend time with people who accept you. Autistic community can help us accept other autistic people, and that makes it easier to accept ourselves for who we are.

Autistic community creates autistic pride. We deserve to feel proud of who we are!

Autistic Community History

There have always been autistic people as long as humans have been around. We have always found each other and spent time together. But 30 years ago, something new happened! The internet got started, and people went online. This made it easier for autistic people to find each other. Autistic people first started talking to each other online, and soon, autistic people started meeting in person. After that, autistic people started forming our own groups. We started talking about being autistic, and taught others about autism. Since then, autistic people have made lots of communities! Some autistic communities are on the internet, and some meet in-person.

Finding Autistic Community Near You

There are a lot of groups where autistic people hang out together, and there might be one near you. These can be great places to meet other autistic people!

Some of these groups might not have what you are looking for. Some of them are run by non-autistic people, and they might try to make autistic people act "normal." Always be careful when looking for groups. Here are some ways to tell if a group will work for you:

Who is in charge?

Is the group run by autistic people or someone else? Do non-disabled people help with the group? Do they tell everyone what to do? It's always best if autistic people decide what their group does.

What is the goal of the group?

Is it for autistic people to hang out? Is it to do disability advocacy? You can choose a group that does things you're interested in.

Is the goal to teach us how to act non-autistic? We shouldn't have to act non-autistic to meet other autistic people. It is a big problem if the group is not a safe place to be autistic.

Who can join?

Is it just autistic people? Can non-autistic people join, too? Both kinds of groups can be good, but some autistic people want groups that are just for us. Pick a group that works for you!

Here are some places you can find autistic communities:

- **Local meetup groups.** Some autistic groups meet using a site called **meetup.com**.

    You can search "autism group" on that website to find groups near you.

- **Autistic Self Advocacy Network affiliate groups.** ASAN has a list of groups that we work with. You can check and see if there is one near you. The list is at **autisticadvocacy.org/affiliates**

- **People First groups.** Most states have People First groups for people with intellectual and developmental disabilities. People First groups work on self-advocacy and fight for our rights. You can find a list of People First groups at **peoplefirst.org/usa**

- **College groups.** Some colleges have groups for disabled people. Some groups include all disabled people, while others are just for autistic people. Most colleges have a website for groups. People who aren't students can't always get to these websites. If you are a student, it is a good place to look, but if not, you can try to call or email the colleges and ask.

Sometimes there are conferences for autistic people. A **conference** is when people from many different places get together and talk about a specific thing, like autism. Conferences usually happen once a year.

Autistic Community Online

There are a lot of autistic people online, and many autistic people talk online using social media.

Social media are websites that people use to talk to each other, like:

- Facebook
- Twitter
- Tumblr
- Instagram
- Reddit

You can find other autistic people by searching on these websites. You can look up words like "autism" or "neurodiversity" or "#ActuallyAutistic." Sometimes, non-autistic people will use these words online, and say bad things about autistic people. You might find these people when you search social media websites, but you should ignore them. Keep looking and you'll find actually autistic people.

Creating Your Own Autistic Community

If you still can't find an autistic community, you can create your own! The Autistic Self Advocacy Network (ASAN) also has tools to help you make a community. To find the tools, look at the end of this chapter.

Who Is Left Out?

Autistic communities sometimes leave some people out. People of color can get left out. Women, transgender, and non-binary people can get left out. Poor people might not be able to afford to come. People with other disabilities might get left out, too.

Sometimes people are left out on purpose.

For example:

> Bob runs a group for autistic people. He says the group is only for "high-functioning" people, so autistic people with intellectual disabilities get left out. This is bad!

But groups can also leave people out by accident.

For example:

> May runs a group for autistic people. She says the group is for all autistic people, but at the group, most of the people are in college. They talk using long, hard words, and get mad when people ask them to use shorter words. Autistic people with intellectual disabilities stop coming to the group. May doesn't want to leave people out, but her group isn't accessible for everyone.

There are also problems in society that make some autistic people get left out. These problems happened before Bob or May started their groups, but they are still problems.

Being left out happens for a lot of reasons. Here are some:

1: Society has wrong ideas about who can be autistic.

Remember, doctors still miss a lot of autistic people, like women and people of color. These people might not get an autism diagnosis, so they might not know they are autistic. That will make it hard for them to find your group.

Most autistic people in TV shows, books, and movies are white boys and men, even though most autistic people are not white boys and men. There are not a lot of autistic women in TV shows, books, and movies, so autistic women don't see examples of autistic people like them. There are not a lot of autistic people of color in TV shows, books, and movies, so autistic people of color don't see examples of autistic people like them. This can make it harder for them to realize they are autistic.

Non-autistic people also see movies, TV, and books, so they also mostly see autistic white men. Doctors see movies, television, and books, so they may think that only white men can be autistic. They might not diagnose women or people of color with autism.

Because of this, your group might just be white autistic men, and other autistic people might not feel like they belong in the group. Groups need to find ways to help everyone feel like they belong.

2: Some groups leave out people who don't have a diagnosis.

Not all autistic people have a diagnosis since it can be hard to get a diagnosis. Also, some people don't want a diagnosis. Some groups ban people who don't have a diagnosis, so those groups leave a lot of people out.

3: Some groups aren't accessible.

You need to think about making your group accessible. Different autistic people have different needs. For example, some autistic people have a hard time with loud noises. If your group has lots of people talking at once, it might not be accessible. Some non-speaking autistic people need more time to write out their thoughts. If people in your group talk too fast, non-speaking people might get left out.

Some autistic people have other disabilities. An autistic person might also use a wheelchair, so groups need to meet in an accessible building. Some autistic people are Deaf, so groups need to make sure to get a sign language interpreter.

When your group isn't accessible, people get left out.

4: Some autistic people think they're better than other autistic people.

There are a lot of different ways to be autistic, and no way is better than any other way.

Some autistic people talk, while others don't talk. Some autistic people only need a little help, while others need help all the time. Some autistic people also have intellectual disabilities, while others don't. This is all okay! All of these autistic people belong in the autistic community.

But society tells us it is not okay to need help. Society tells us it is not okay to have an intellectual disability, and it's not okay to be non-speaking. Some autistic people believe these things. They think it's bad to have intellectual disabilities, to be non-speaking, or to need a lot of help. They look down on autistic people who have intellectual disabilities, are non-speaking, or need a lot of help. They might treat these people badly or not let them into their group.

Sometimes, people don't say these ideas out loud, and show them with their actions instead. They might say that anyone can come to their group, but get mad if someone needs extra help. They might say they care about all autistic people, then make fun of people who can't use big words.

Autistic groups should include all autistic people. All autistic people are important, and deserve rights and respect.

---

5. Autistic people can discriminate too!

Lots of different kinds of people are autistic. Some autistic people are also:

- People of color
- Women
- Trans
- Non-binary
- Gay
- Muslim

- Jewish

- Lots of other things!

Society discriminates against lots of different kinds of people, and autistic people are a part of society. That means autistic people can also discriminate. Sometimes, autistic people discriminate against other autistic people. An autistic man might discriminate against an autistic woman, or a white autistic person might discriminate against an autistic person of color.

For example:

> Yolanda is an autistic woman of color. She goes to an autism group, and talks about a time that someone was racist to her. The other people at the group tell her to talk about something else. They say her story isn't important because it isn't about autism. They make Yolanda feel bad about being a person of color, so she leaves the group and does not come back.

Discrimination keeps people out of groups. If your group discriminates, people might feel left out and stop coming to your group. If you want your group to include everyone, don't discriminate.

What can you do?

There are lots of ways to leave people out of the autistic community. You might be doing some of those things, but don't worry! You can stop doing them. Here are some things you can try.

1: Pay attention to what you think, what you do, and how you treat other autistic people.

You might be doing things that leave people out. You might not mean to do them, and you may have never realized you were doing them. That is normal. Now that you know, you can stop doing them.

2: Look at your autistic communities and ask yourself who is missing.

Is everyone you follow on Twitter white? Does your group only have men in it? Who are you missing? Figure out who is missing, and think about why and how they got left out. Then, you should try to fix those things.

3: Learn about ways to help everyone feel like they belong.

Talk to different kinds of people, and learn what makes them feel like they belong. Ask them where you can learn more. You can also learn more online. Lots of people are trying to learn more about these things, and there is always more to learn. It's important to keep learning.

Chapter Eight Resources

You can find the links to these resources at
autismacceptance.com/book/chapter-8-resources

- Autism On Television Needs More Diverse Representation - by Alaina Leary

- Video: Intersectionality 101 - by Teaching Tolerance

- How to Make Your Social Justice Events Accessible to the Disability Community: A Checklist - by s.e. Smith

Being An Ally

An ally is someone who isn't autistic that helps autistic people. They listen to autistic people and help us get what we need.

This chapter will cover the basics of being an ally. This chapter is for non-autistic people who want to be allies. You might be our family, our friends, or you might just be interested. Autistic people might be interested in this chapter, too. Every autistic person has different needs, and we can all learn how to be better allies to each other.

The Basics of Being An Ally

There are lots of ways to have a brain. Some people are autistic, while some people have other disabilities that change their brain. Other people don't have disabilities that change their brain.

That's fine. No brain is better than any other brain.

Autism is a disability, and disability is a normal part of being a human. You can learn more about disability in Chapter 5. That chapter can help you understand disability and be a better ally.

Autistic people are part of the disability rights movement. We have a right to be ourselves, and to be in the same world as everyone else. Being an ally means helping us fight for our rights.

Here are some things everyone can do to be an ally to autistic people:

Learn about autism from autistic people.

Autistic people know the most about autism, since we know what it is like to be autistic. Non-autistic people will never know what it is like to be autistic, so they should learn about autism by talking to us. Ask autistic people first when you have questions about autism.

Here are some places where autistic people talk about autism:

- The Autistic Self Advocacy Network
- The Autistic Women and Nonbinary Network
- The Thinking Person's Guide to Autism

- #AskingAutistics on social media. People add #AskingAutistics to their posts to ask autistic people questions.

Respect our privacy.

Autistic people have a right to privacy. We should be able to choose what people know about us. We should have control over what pictures and videos are shared of us. We should have control over the stories people tell about us. We should get to decide what things about us get shared and what things about us are private.

A lot of parents take pictures of their kids. This can be a good thing, but some parents take pictures of their kids doing private things. They may take pictures of their kid in the bath, or having a meltdown. Then, they share the pictures with everyone on the internet. Autistic people deserve privacy, even when we are kids. We need even more privacy when we're having a hard time.

Sometimes, autistic people will teach others about autism. We might share private things about our lives to help people learn. That doesn't mean we want to share those things all the time, or share these things with everyone. Don't repeat private things an autistic person tells you, and ask first if you want to share our story with someone else.

Autistic people also have a right not to share private things. Autistic people talk about autism all the time, and some people ask us private questions about our lives. We have a right to not answer these questions. We should still get to talk about autism. We shouldn't have to share when we were toilet trained, when we were diagnosed, or whether or not we hurt ourselves. We get to decide what we want to share.

Autistic people you are close to might tell you private things. This is a normal part of being family or friends. You shouldn't tell other people about things we say in private. The rules are the same for us as when a non-autistic person tells you a secret.

Respect our bodies.

Autistic people have a right to control our own bodies. A lot of times, people don't respect this right. They might touch us without asking, try to change how we move, or do things to our bodies that we don't like. A big part of being an ally is respecting our rights, and that means making sure we are in charge of our bodies.

One way to respect our bodies is to let us stim. If you don't know what stimming is, go to Chapter 3. All people stim, but when autistic people stim, some people try to stop us. This is wrong. Stimming is a big part of our lives, and allies should make sure we can keep stimming.

Respect our communication.

Everyone communicates in different ways, and allies help us find ways to communicate.

Some autistic people talk, and others don't. Some autistic people talk differently than non-autistic people. Some of us use AAC. If you don't know what AAC is, go to Chapter 3.

Some people use AAC all the time, while others go back and forth between AAC and talking.

Some people repeat things they've heard before, or talk for a long time. Some people use words that don't seem to make sense, or show what they think by how they act.

No matter how we communicate, we all have something to say. Being an ally means listening to us, and taking what we say seriously. It means making sure other people listen to us.

Believe in us.

Autistic people learn, think, feel, and grow, just like all people do. Sometimes, other people forget that we are people. This happens a lot to non-speaking people and people with intellectual disabilities. Other people say that we can't learn, think, feel, or grow. This is wrong!

An ally remembers that we are people. An ally knows that we have thoughts, that we are listening, and that we can learn. An ally works hard to communicate with us. They help us find ways to show what we think and learn, and how we feel.

Believing in us means making sure we get to make choices. It means giving us lots of chances to do different things. It means treating us the way other people our age are treated. It means letting us do things in the way that works best for us.

Believing in us also means giving us the support we need. All of us have things we need help with. Allies believe we can live good lives with the right help, and they help us get the support we need to live good lives.

Believing us means taking us seriously when we ask for help. Sometimes, it might not look like we need help, but we still do.

For example:

> Chauncey is autistic. He is in middle school. He falls on some stairs and hurts his leg. He goes to the school nurse and says "My leg hurts." Chauncey isn't frowning or crying, so the nurse says to Chauncey, "You don't look like you're in pain." The nurse doesn't help Chauncey, but later, his parents figure out that Chauncey broke his leg. The nurse should have believed Chauncey.

Don't assume things about autistic people.

Every day, we assume things about other people. We look at how other people act, and then we judge them. For example, someone might not make eye contact, so we assume they are lying. Someone might be frowning, so we assume they are upset. Someone might put their head on the table, so we assume they are tired. Someone might face away from us when we are talking, so we assume they aren't listening.

But people do things for lots of different reasons. If someone doesn't make eye contact, they might not like eye contact, or they could be blind. If someone is frowning, that might just be how their face looks, or they might be happy, but not be able to smile. If someone puts their head on the table, they might be dizzy, or they might not have strong neck muscles. If someone faces away from us when we are talking, they might be shy, or they might focus better if they aren't looking at you.

Non-autistic people assume things about us from how we act, and that's a big problem! Autistic people experience the world differently than other people, and that means we might act differently than others. Or, we might do the same thing as other people, but for different reasons.

Everyone has reasons for doing what they do, so don't assume all those reasons are the same for everyone. You might not trust someone because they don't make eye contact. You might get mad at someone for frowning when they should be happy. These things happen to autistic people all the time. They don't happen because people are trying to be mean to us, but they happen because people assume things about us.

An ally tries not to assume things. Try to notice when you assume things about people. If you see someone talking to themselves, what do you think? If you see someone stimming, what do you think? If you see someone having a meltdown, what do you think? This can help you assume things less.

There's only one way to know why someone acts how they do, and that way is to ask them! Ask us if you aren't sure why we do certain things.

Talk about autism respectfully.

The way we talk about autism matters, and using different words changes how other people treat us. An ally is careful to talk about autism respectfully. They pay attention to their words.

Talking about autism respectfully isn't just about using the right words, but there are still some words that are important to say or not say. There are also some ideas that help us and some that hurt us. Here are some tips for how to talk about autism respectfully.

Ask autistic people how we want you to talk about us. Ask us if we want to be called "autistic" or "someone with autism."

Don't use pictures of puzzle pieces to mean autism. Some people think that autism is a big mystery, and see autistic people as puzzles that need to be solved. So, they started using puzzle pieces to mean autism.

Someone did a study about autism and puzzle pieces. They talked to people about autism, then showed people puzzle pieces to mean autism. Then they asked people what they thought about autism, and found out the puzzle pieces made people think autism is bad. Autistic people don't like it when people use puzzle pieces to mean autism because we are people, not puzzles.

Sometimes, people will say that someone is "low-functioning", "high-functioning", has "severe autism", or "mild autism". These words aren't helpful, and you shouldn't do this. We talk more about why you shouldn't say these words in Chapter 1. Instead, just say what you mean. If you mean that someone is non-speaking, say that. If you mean that someone has an intellectual disability, say that. If you mean that someone has certain support needs, say that.

Never say that anyone is "retarded" or a "retard." This word gets used to hurt people with intellectual disabilities, and you should never say this word to anyone.

Some people say that "everyone's a little bit autistic." because some things that autistic people do are things that everyone does. For example, everyone stims, but stimming is more important for autistic people. Saying "everyone's a little bit autistic" can hurt us because people use it to say autism isn't really a disability. That means people might not help us get what we need. It's okay to talk about things that everyone does, but don't say "everyone's a little bit autistic".

An ally makes sure their words don't make autism seem bad or sad, and their words don't make autistic people seem broken or scary. That's already what a lot of people think about autism, and an ally's job is to change how other people think about autism.

An ally always remembers that autistic people can hear them. When you say bad things about autism, it hurts us. An ally talks about autism like there is an autistic person standing right behind them.

Partner with autistic people.

Autistic people work in every job you can think of. We are scientists, researchers, writers, artists, and dancers. Wherever you go, there are autistic people, and no matter what job you do, autistic people do that job, too.

Remember the motto "Nothing about us, without us!" If an ally works on projects about autism, they make sure they work with autistic people on these projects. Autistic people should always be a part of projects about autism. It does not matter what kind of project it is, since autistic people will always have important ideas to add.

It's not enough to just have us there when you do your project. You need to listen to us, make sure we understand what you are doing, and give us time to share our thoughts. You need to take our thoughts seriously, and change parts of your project that might hurt us.

An ally works with autistic people at every step of the project. An ally asks autistic people to help plan the project, and gives us chances to share ideas while the project happens. Don't wait until your project is finished to ask us what we think. It's too late to change anything if you wait until the end, so you wouldn't really be listening to us.

Here is an example of a good project:

> Camila is writing a book. Her book has an autistic person in it. Camila talks to autistic people about her book, and lets autistic people read the book before anyone else. Autistic people tell her that parts of the book make autism seem like a bad thing. Camila changes those parts of the book, and pays the autistic people for helping her.

Here is an example of a bad project:

> Mario is autistic, and he is a well-known self-advocate in his town. Isaac is non-autistic, and he is planning an autism conference. He gets a group of people to help him plan the conference, but all of the people are non-autistic, except for Mario. Mario tries to make sure the conference is good for autistic people, but Isaac doesn't listen to Mario.
>
> The conference ends up being bad for autistic people, but Isaac thinks the conference was fine. When some autistic people try to tell Isaac that it was bad, Isaac says, "Mario helped plan the conference. It isn't my fault you didn't like it!"

Learn from your mistakes.

Everyone makes mistakes. As an ally, you will make mistakes, and you might hurt autistic people by accident. Your advocacy might not work.

Sometimes, autistic people will tell you about mistakes you made, or you might find out on your own. Making mistakes is a normal part of being an ally. It is important to know when you made a mistake so you can make it better. You can figure out how to fix your mistakes, and keep trying to be a good ally.

Some mistakes will be easy to fix. For example, if you use a word that hurts us, it is easy to stop using that word. Some mistakes will be harder to fix. For example:

You might have a job that hurts autistic people. The job might try and make us look less autistic, which makes it harder for us to be ourselves. You might need to change your job.

Being an ally sometimes means doing hard things. Autistic people understand that, since we have to do hard things all the time. It is hard to live in a society that hurts us, so it is important that our allies work hard to change that.

A note for families

Families can be strong allies for their autistic family members. Many years ago, parents of disabled kids started getting together. They worked to close institutions, and fought for their kids to get support in the community. Parents are still fighting today for the rights of their kids. You can be a part of that fight, too!

Families can make a big difference for their family members. You can support your autistic family member to have a good life, and help fight for our rights. You can make sure your family is a safe place for us, and help other families be allies, too.

There is some information and tools just for you at the end of this chapter.

Chapter Nine Resources

You can find the links to these resources at
autismacceptance.com/book/chapter-9-resources

- Don't Mourn for Us - by Jim Sinclair

- Checklist of Neurotypical Privilege - by Bev Harp

- Autistikids

- In the Loop About Neurodiversity

- Learn From Autistics

- Thinking Person's Guide to Autism

- Think Inclusive

- Parenting Autistic Children with Love & Acceptance

Words To Know

Ableism

Discrimination against disabled people.

Accessibility

When disabled people can easily use something. We can easily get around somewhere. We feel like we belong there.

Accommodations

Changes that make things easier for disabled people. They help us get the same things as non-disabled people.

Allies

Non-autistic people who want to help autistic people. All sorts of people can be allies.

Americans with Disabilities Act (ADA)

A law that gives people with disabilities lots of different rights. People say it is the biggest disability rights law in the United States.

Augmentative and Alternative Communication (AAC)

Using something other than talking to communicate.

Cisgender

When your gender is the same as people thought when you were born.

Communication

How we show others what we want and need. Everybody communicates!

Conference

When people from many different places get together. They all talk about a specific thing, like autism.

Developmental disability

A type of disability that begins when someone is very young. Autism is a developmental disability. So is cerebral palsy.

Diagnosis

When a doctor says you are autistic.

Disability rights movement

When disabled people fight back against ableism. We work to change society to be better for disabled people.

Discrimination

Treating people badly because of who they are

Echolalia

Repeating things that you have heard before, like a line in a TV show.

Executive functioning

A group of skills that help people stay on track. Following a plan is an example of executive functioning.

Fair Housing Act

A law that makes sure people with disabilities have housing rights.

Fine motor skills

Small movements, like writing or tying your shoes.

Functioning labels

Words that try and show different "types" of autism. "High functioning" and "low functioning" are some examples of functioning labels.

Gross motor skills

Big movements, like running or swimming.

Guardian

Someone who can make legal decisions for a person with disabilities.

IDEA

A law that gives rights to students with disabilities.

Identity-first language

Putting the word for a disability before the word "person". "Autistic people" is identity-first language. So is "Disabled people".

IEP

A plan that schools need to make for each student with a disability. The plan helps set goals for students with disabilities.

Intellectual disabilities

Disabilities that affect how you learn and think. People with intellectual disabilities might learn more slowly.

Legal rights

Rights that the law gives to you.

Meltdowns

When an autistic person gets too stressed and can't control their feelings. They might scream, cry, or run away.

Motor skills

How people control the way their body moves.

Neurodiversity

The idea that humans have all kinds of brains.

There is no such thing as a "normal" brain.

Neurodiversity movement

A part of the disability rights movement. It says that people with all kinds of brains should be accepted in society.

Non-binary

When someone isn't just a boy or a girl.

Non-speaking

People who don't talk with their mouths.

Nonverbal communication

Communication that doesn't use language. Body language and eye contact are examples of nonverbal communication.

Olmstead

A court case about people with disabilities in institutions. It says people with disabilities have a right to live in the community.

Peer pressure

When people around you tell you to do something. You might do that thing even if you don't want to.

People of color

People who are not white. For example, black people are people of color.

Person-first language

Putting the word "person" before the word for a disability. "People with autism" is person-first language. So is "People with disabilities".

Processing

How your brain thinks about and reacts to things.

Protection & Advocacy Agencies (P&As)

Groups in each state that help people with disabilities fight for our rights. They make sure states follow disability laws.

Rehab Act

A law that makes rules for programs the government pays for.

Scripting

When people plan ahead of time what they want to say.

Section 504

The part of the Rehab Act that talks about disability rights.

Section 504 Plan

A plan that says what a student needs to be able to learn.

Self-advocacy

Standing up for yourself so you get what you need.

Self-advocacy movement

When people with intellectual and developmental disabilities fight for our rights. It is a part of the disability rights movement.

Self-diagnosis

When you figure out that you are autistic.

Sensory processing

How you think about and understand your senses.

Shutdowns

When someone stops being able to do anything. They might not be able to talk or move.

Socializing

How we get along with other people.

Social media

Websites that people use to talk to each other.

Society

A big group of communities. A society usually has rules and people in charge.

Special interests

Very strong interests that autistic people have.

Stimming

Moving in the same way over and over again. Everyone stims, but autistic people stim more than other people.

Supported decision-making

When a disabled person gets help making decisions. People can use supported decision-making instead of getting a guardian.

Support needs

The things autistic people need help with.

Supreme Court

The U.S. court that has the final say on how laws work.

Transgender

When your gender is different than people thought when you were born.

Transition plan

A plan that helps disabled students decide what they will do after high school.

Vaccines

Shots you get to help you not get sick. For example, the flu shot is a vaccine.

CPSIA information can be obtained
at www.ICGtesting.com
Printed in the USA
BVHW081932251120
594000BV00006B/607

9 781938 800085